To Carrie Rodd

AQUARIUS

A guide to living your best astrological life

STELLA ANDROMEDA

ILLUSTRATED BY EVI O. STUDIO

Hardie Grant

BOOKS

Introduction 7

I.

Get to Know Aquarius

II.

The Aquarius Deep Dive

III.

Give Me More

Introduction

Inscribed on the forecourt of the ancient Greek temple of
Apollo at Delphi are the words 'know thyself'. This is one of
the 147 Delphic maxims, or rules to live by, attributed to Apollo
himself, and was later extended by the philosopher Socrates to
the sentence, 'The unexamined life is not worth living.'

People seek a variety of ways of knowing themselves, of
coming to terms with life and trying to find ways to understand
the challenges of human existence, often through therapy
or belief systems like organised religion. These are ways in
which we strive to understand the relationships we have with
ourselves and others better, seeking out particular tools that
enable us to do so.

As far as systems of understanding human nature and
experience go, astrology has much to offer through its symbolic
use of the constellations of the heavens, the depictions of the
zodiac signs, the planets and their energetic effects. Many
people find accessing this information and harnessing its
potential a useful way of thinking about how to manage
their lives more effectively.

What is astrology?

In simple terms, astrology is the study and interpretation of how the planets can influence us, and the world in which we live, through an understanding of their positions at a specific place in time. The practice of astrology relies on a combination of factual knowledge of the characteristics of these positions and their psychological interpretation.

Astrology is less of a belief system and more of a tool for living, from which ancient and established wisdom can be drawn. Any of us can learn to use astrology, not so much for divination or telling the future, but as a guidebook that provides greater insight and a more thoughtful way of approaching life. Timing is very much at the heart of astrology, and knowledge of planetary configurations and their relationship to each other at specific moments in time can assist in helping us with the timing of some of our life choices and decisions.

Knowing when major life shifts can occur – because of particular planetary configurations such as a Saturn return (see page 103) or Mercury retrograde (see page 104) – or what it means to have Venus in your seventh house (see pages 85 and 98), while recognising the specific characteristics of your sign, are all tools that you can use to your advantage. Knowledge is power, and astrology can be a very powerful supplement to approaching life's ups and downs and any relationships we form along the way.

The 12 signs of the zodiac

Each sign of the zodiac has a range of recognisable
characteristics, shared by people born under that sign. This
is your Sun sign, which you probably already know – and the
usual starting point from which we each begin to explore
our own astrological paths. Sun sign characteristics can be
strongly exhibited in an individual's make-up; however, this
is only part of the picture.

Usually, how we appear to others is tempered by the influence
of other factors – and these are worth bearing in mind. Your
ascendant sign is equally important, as is the positioning of your
Moon. You can also look to your opposite sign to see what your
Sun sign may need a little more of, to balance its characteristics.

After getting to know your Sun sign in the first part of this
book, you might want to dive into the Give Me More section
(see pages 74–105) to start to explore all the particulars of your
birth chart. These will give you far greater insight into the myriad
astrological influences that may play out in your life.

Sun signs

It takes 365 (and a quarter, to be precise) days for the Earth to orbit the Sun and in so doing, the Sun appears to us to spend a month travelling through each sign of the zodiac. Your Sun sign is therefore an indication of the sign that the Sun was travelling through at the time of your birth. Knowing what Sun signs you and your family, friends and lovers are provides you with just the beginning of the insights into character and personality that astrology can help you discover.

On the cusp

For those for whom a birthday falls close to the end of one Sun sign and the beginning of another, it's worth knowing what time you were born. There's no such thing, astrologically, as being 'on the cusp' – because the signs begin at a specific time on a specific date, although this can vary a little year on year. If you are not sure, you'll need to know your birth date, birth time and birth place to work out accurately to which Sun sign you belong. Once you have these, you can consult an astrologer or run your details through an online astrology site program (see page 108) to give you the most accurate birth chart possible.

Taurus

The bull

★

21 APRIL–20 MAY

Aries

The ram

★

21 MARCH–20 APRIL

Astrologically the first sign of the zodiac, Aries appears alongside the vernal (or spring) equinox. A cardinal fire sign, depicted by the ram, it is the sign of beginnings and ruled by planet Mars, which represents a dynamic ability to meet challenges energetically and creatively. Its opposite sign is airy Libra.

Grounded, sensual and appreciative of bodily pleasures, Taurus is a fixed earth sign endowed by its ruling planet Venus with grace and a love of beauty, despite its depiction as a bull. Generally characterised by an easy and uncomplicated, if occasionally stubborn, approach to life, Taurus' opposite sign is watery Scorpio.

Gemini

The twins

✦

21 MAY–20 JUNE

A mutable air sign symbolised by the twins, Gemini tends to see both sides of an argument, its speedy intellect influenced by its ruling planet Mercury. Tending to fight shy of commitment, this sign also epitomises a certain youthfulness of attitude. Its opposite sign is fiery Sagittarius.

Cancer

The crab

✦

21 JUNE–21 JULY

Depicted by the crab and the tenacity of its claws, Cancer is a cardinal water sign, emotional and intuitive, its sensitivity protected by its shell. Ruled by the maternal Moon, the shell also represents the security of home, to which Cancer is committed. Its opposite sign is earthy Capricorn.

Leo

The lion

★

A fixed fire sign, ruled by the Sun, Leo loves to shine and is an idealist at heart, positive and generous to a fault. Depicted by the lion, Leo can roar with pride and be confident and uncompromising, with a great faith and trust in humanity. Its opposite sign is airy Aquarius.

Virgo

The virgin

★

22 AUGUST–21 SEPTEMBER

Traditionally represented as a maiden or virgin, this mutable earth sign is observant, detail oriented and tends towards self-sufficiency. Ruled by Mercury, Virgo benefits from a sharp intellect that can be self-critical, while often being very health conscious. Its opposite sign is watery Pisces.

Scorpio

The scorpion

22 OCTOBER–21 NOVEMBER

Given to intense feelings, as befits a fixed water sign, Scorpio is depicted by the scorpion – linking it to the rebirth that follows death – and is ruled by both Pluto and Mars. With a strong spirituality and deep emotions, Scorpio needs security to transform its strength. Its opposite sign is earthy Taurus.

Libra

The scales

22 SEPTEMBER–21 OCTOBER

A cardinal air sign, ruled by Venus, Libra is all about beauty, balance (as depicted by the scales) and harmony in its rather romanticised, ideal world. With a strong aesthetic sense, Libra can be both arty and crafty, but also likes fairness and can be very diplomatic. Its opposite sign is fiery Aries.

Sagittarius

The archer

✳

22 NOVEMBER–21 DECEMBER

Depicted by the archer, Sagittarius is a mutable fire sign that's all about travel and adventure, in body or mind, and is very direct in approach. Ruled by the benevolent Jupiter, Sagittarius is optimistic with lots of ideas; liking a free rein, but with a tendency to generalise. Its opposite sign is airy Gemini.

Capricorn

The goat

✳

22 DECEMBER–20 JANUARY

Ruled by Saturn, Capricorn is a cardinal earth sign associated with hard work and depicted by the sure-footed and sometimes playful goat. Trustworthy and unafraid of commitment, Capricorn is often very self-sufficient and has the discipline for the freelance working life. Its opposite sign is the watery Cancer.

Aquarius

The water carrier

21 JANUARY–19 FEBRUARY

Confusingly, given its depiction by the water carrier, Aquarius is a fixed air sign ruled by the unpredictable Uranus, sweeping away old ideas with innovative thinking. Tolerant, open-minded and all about humanity, its vision is social with a conscience. Its opposite sign is fiery Leo.

Pisces

The fish

★

20 FEBRUARY–20 MARCH

Acutely responsive to its surroundings, Pisces is a mutable water sign depicted by two fish, swimming in opposite directions, sometimes confusing fantasy with reality. Ruled by Neptune, its world is fluid, imaginative and empathetic, often picking up on the moods of others. Its opposite sign is earthy Virgo.

Get to

I.

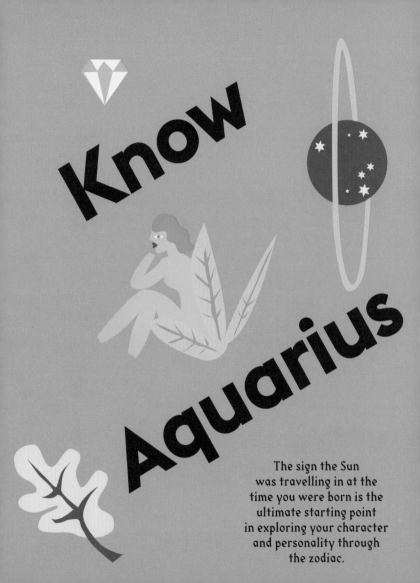

Know

Aquarius

The sign the Sun
was travelling in at the
time you were born is the
ultimate starting point
in exploring your character
and personality through
the zodiac.

Fixed air sign, depicted by the water bearer.

Ruled by Uranus, Aquarius is associated with disruption and the unexpected; with innovation and invention.

OPPOSITE SIGN

Leo

STATEMENT OF SELF

'I know.'

Lucky colour

Blue, the shade of the sky and the air above us, from which water (representing life) can rain down. Wear bright blue colours when you need a psychological boost and additional courage. If you don't want to be ostentatious with a strong colour, choose darker or lighter tones for accessories – shoes, gloves, socks, hat, or even underwear.

Lucky day

Wednesday. The middle of the working week for most of us, this links to the old-English deity Woden, so it's actually Woden's day *(Wōdnesdæg)*. Woden's Roman equivalent is the airy Mercury of Aquarian influence, which we see more obviously in the French for Wednesday, *Mercredi*.

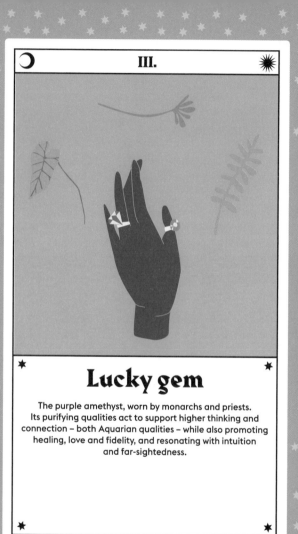

Lucky gem

The purple amethyst, worn by monarchs and priests.
Its purifying qualities act to support higher thinking and
connection – both Aquarian qualities – while also promoting
healing, love and fidelity, and resonating with intuition
and far-sightedness.

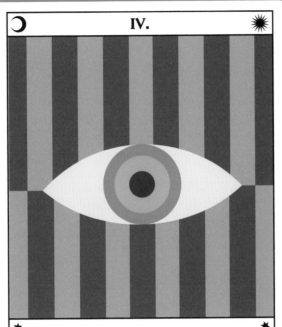

Locations

Countries that link to the qualities of Aquarius include
Sri Lanka, Finland, Ethiopia and Russia, while the cities
of Tallinn, Buenos Aires, Brighton, Salzburg and Stockholm
also resonate with the Aquarian energy for innovation,
ideas and progressive attitudes.

Holidays

Highly adaptable and independently minded, Aquarius is happy to travel far beyond the beaten track to visit new and interesting places. Young at heart and happy to fly long haul, Aquarius loves both wide open spaces and the bustle of cities, and backpacking around places like India will appeal to them whatever their age.

Flowers

The exotic orchid, representing luxury and refinement, resonates with the Aquarian qualities of the spiritual connection that can exist between people. It is a flower also associated with both mental strength and male virility.

Trees

As Aquarius' thought and innovation bears fruit,
so do those trees that rely on water to grow and bear fruit,
like the apple, pear, cherry, mango and orange. Fruit trees
also lend themselves to innovation, producing hybrid
fruits like the tangelo and the plumcot.

Pets

As might be expected of an air sign, a bird is an attractive pet for Aquarius, and because of their sociability, an electric blue-coloured love bird or two, or an exotic, talking Mynah bird might just fit the bill.

Parties

Social Aquarius loves to party and particularly loves informal, spontaneous gatherings. To them, a stranger is just a friend they haven't yet met and what better place to meet than at a party! When it comes to theme or location, expect the unexpected. Cocktails using Blue Curaçao – like a Blue Lagoon or Blue Hawaiian – might contribute to the Aquarian party spirit.

Aquarius characteristics

Independent, thoughtful, innovative and tolerant are all key words associated with Aquarius, whose capacity for ideas and adventure means they are never boring. Those born under this Sun sign are also considered to be humanitarian and egalitarian: they are concerned with humanity as a whole and with big ideas for improving life for everyone, in practical rather than spiritual ways. Freedom of thought, expression and movement are all dear to the Aquarian heart and they will avidly support free speech, freedom of information and human rights. The freedom to be oneself lies at the heart of Aquarian philosophy, which is extended to one and all – and with love. Which is also why Aquarius probably has the widest, most diverse, circle of friends and, as depicted by the water bearer, they happily 'go with the flow'.

Aquarius also embraces the innovation of new technology, the internet and global communication with all its upsides and downsides. Communicative, with a magpie curiosity for ideas and connections, there's a cool airiness but overriding friendliness about Aquarius, which makes them popular. Thanks to Uranus, there's a breadth of vision that also makes Aquarius very good at the big picture. They don't tend to sweat the small stuff, but problem-solve in interesting and unpredictable ways. Aquarius is the friend with the big ideas, but actually doing the graft to deliver on these is a lesser inclination. Talking the talk is one thing, walking the walk a different proposition for someone with their head (almost literally) in the clouds, so it's here that harnessing all those friends and acquaintances to deal with the minutiae is an important part of any Aquarius plan.

That slight emotional distance that is so characteristic of the sign can sometimes be seen as aloofness. But Aquarius makes a good and tolerant friend, although sometimes they find that a closer intimacy is less easy. When they do get close and commit, however, Aquarius is extremely loyal, and they offer *unconditional* love and support, which is unusual. That their commitment comes with no strings attached can sometimes be misinterpreted as a desire for freedom, so Aquarius needs to make it clear that unconditional doesn't mean uncommitted. It's as well for Aquarius to use their thoughtfulness and verbal ability to communicate their deeper feelings, as these may not always be immediately obvious.

FANNING THE AIR

The key characteristics of any
Sun sign can be balanced out
(or sometimes reinforced) by the
characteristics of other signs in the
same birth chart, particularly those
of the ascendant and the Moon. So
if someone doesn't appear to be
typical of their Sun sign, that's why.
However, those nascent Aquarius
aspects will always be there as
a key influence, informing an
individual's approach to life.

Physical
Aquarius

Aquarius is generally strong, healthy and quite active, with an enquiring eye and interesting take on the world around them. Their activity may be more mental than physical because, although outgoing, Aquarius also likes nothing better than to sit and talk and can sometimes carry some extra weight as a result of this more sedentary attitude. Generally, though, Aquarius has a youthful appearance that appears fleet of foot because their whole approach to life is so forward looking. Their movements tend to be well co-ordinated and energetic, as if they are always on the point of dashing off to their next adventure.

Health

The sign of Aquarius is associated with the circulation system of the body, the blood and the lymphatic system, and also with the lower legs from the knees to the ankles. Because they are very much in their heads, Aquarius don't always give their bodies much attention until something goes wrong and, even then, there's a tendency to disregard it. And although they have a generally healthy constitution, when they do fall ill it tends to come on quickly and unexpectedly, but they also tend to recover equally fast, which is the nature of those ruled by unpredictable Uranus. A strong mental attitude means that they expect to overcome physical health problems quickly, and they usually do.

Exercise

Keeping the leg muscles strong and active will also help support the knees and ankles and the circulation in the legs (avoiding problems like varicose veins). Aquarius doesn't mind the gym, because what interests them most is in their heads, and they can think things through there.

How Aquarius communicates

Communication is to Aquarius as necessary as the air they breathe, and they are always happy to share their thoughts and ideas. They tend to think before they speak and are often very gifted in expressing their ideas, taking their time to get it right and convey what they think with accuracy. Aquarius has the ability to be quite objective in their opinions and they often have a lot invested in these.

Although not particularly judgemental, Aquarius often comes across as very sure of their ideas, and even dogmatic on occasion. For Aquarius, arguing is more about intellectual exercise and love of debate, rather than personal attack, but this can make them appear quite uncompromising at times. However, they are generally too easy-going and considerate to let this escalate, being well prepared to agree to differ for the sake of the greater good which is, after all, what Aquarius is all about.

Aquarius careers

As you might imagine for someone with a social conscience and an interest in humanity like Aquarius, they are drawn to occupations that serve other people. Gravitating towards careers like teaching, social work, charity work, human rights and environmental engineering, Aquarius tends to follow their own path into areas where they can work towards positive change for everyone. Even if not obviously working for a humanitarian cause, they will bring an element of this approach to any role.

This is not a Sun sign for whom money is a primary driver, although their very good work ethic may mean they make good money. Innovative technology may well be a factor, too – the person who develops the tsunami warning app that is run out globally and for free? They would probably have strong Aquarian factors in their chart even if it's not their Sun sign. In many ways, Aquarius can be summed up in the phrase 'rebel with a cause' because when it comes to making a contribution to society, they will do it in their own way in whichever career they choose.

How
Aquarius
chimes

From lovers to friends, when it comes to other signs, how does Aquarius get along? Knowledge of other signs and how they interact can be helpful when negotiating relationships, revealed through an understanding of Sun sign characteristics that might chime or chafe. Understanding these through an astrological framework can be really helpful as it can depersonalise potential frictions, taking the sting out of what appears to be in opposition.

Harmonising relationships can sometimes appear to be a problem for Aquarius, but how they chime is partly dependent on what other planetary influences are at play in their personal birth chart, toning down or enhancing aspects of their Sun sign characteristics, especially those that can sometimes clash with other signs.

The Aquarius woman

Independent, friendly and outgoing, the Aquarian woman has a strong romantic streak, but is also distinctly wary of attempts to pin her down, giving her the reputation for being cool in temperament. This is a woman with many far-reaching interests and a lot of friends. Stand in the way of her freedom – of thought, ideas or expression – however, and don't be surprised if she's gone.

NOTABLE AQUARIUS WOMEN

As a Modernist writer, Virginia Woolf changed the nature of literature, while other feminist writers Germaine Greer and Toni Morrison did something similar, years later. Colombian singing star Shakira promotes charitable causes, while Oprah Winfrey is known for her philanthropy. Ellen DeGeneres and Jennifer Aniston are also two highly independent women, successful in their own right.

The Aquarius man

The mind matters as much as the body to this rather cerebral and witty man, but any excessive, over-emotional demands will leave Aquarius cold. He's popular because of his relaxed, generally easy-going and friendly approach to life, but is also one of the most often married of the Sun signs because if he feels trapped, he tends to divorce and move on.

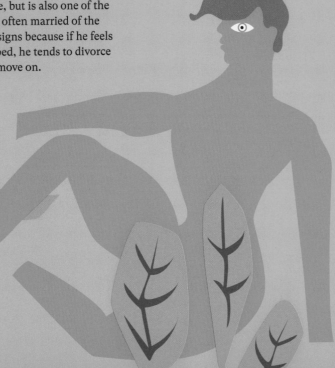

Who love

s whom?

Aquarius & Aries

There's a mutual independence and spontaneity that makes this pair well matched on several fronts, meaning there's often plenty to be shared and enjoyed. But Aries' fiery dominance can sometimes prove a tad overbearing for Aquarius' need for freedom.

Aquarius & Taurus

Earthy, home-loving Taurus tends to find Aquarius' airy independence tricky as it challenges their possessive side, fuelling anxious thoughts in both, while there's also a difference of opinion about the water bearer's all-embracing humanitarian instincts.

Aquarius & Gemini

These two air signs are well matched in temperament and ideas, both keen to live harmoniously and able to tolerate each other's need for freedom. Conversation is a huge part of their relationship and they can talk about just about everything with each other.

Aquarius & Cancer

Cancer's security is rooted in domesticity while Aquarius hardly notices their home surroundings, keen as they are to head off on their next adventure; and this disparity lies at the root of any trouble between these two. Consequently, not an easy match.

Aquarius & Leo

High-spirited and adventurous, they both desire freedom but this can take different routes: Leo's through luxury and an audience while Aquarius wants an equal companion who can rough it when necessary. In this way their opposite natures can clash.

Aquarius & Virgo

Both recognise that they are as equally engaged with the mind as the body, but their goals tend to differ, with Aquarius aiming for brilliantly innovative ideas and Virgo opting for more practical ones, which tends to knock out any compatibility of intellect.

Aquarius & Scorpio

There's a strong attraction here but the unpredictability of Aquarius' nature and their desire for freedom can seriously chafe at Scorpio's intense needs and powerful passions, which Aquarius can find just too much. They need to handle each other with care.

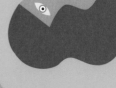

Aquarius & Libra

This pair really know how to enjoy each other and easily spark each other's appetite for fun. While diplomatic Libra has no problem with Aquarius' stubborn streak, they may never quite manage to stabilise their relationship, however, into anything other than a flirtation.

Aquarius & Sagittarius

There's an easy harmony between these two outgoing and independent souls; neither is particularly jealous and both are inventive and exciting enough to hold each other's interest in the bedroom, which is where they are happy to reconnect after time spent apart.

Aquarius &
Aquarius

So comfortable will they be with each other, matched in interest for the new and the unusual, that they could only be happy together. The only downside is that they might not actually spend enough time together to cement any sort of lasting relationship.

Aquarius &
Pisces

Pisces' dreamy, spiritual side probably needs more harnessing in the real world than Aquarius can provide, in spite of the real attraction each holds for the other, which might make it difficult for this relationship to last without compromises on both sides.

Aquarius &
Capricorn

Capricorn's cautious nature tends to bristle at Aquarius' airy disregard for the more practical side of life, which can cause arguments, while there's probably not enough of a sexual spark between them to offset Aquarius' boredom and get further than first base.

Aquarius love-o-meter

Least compatible

Capricorn Cancer Virgo Leo Taurus Pisces

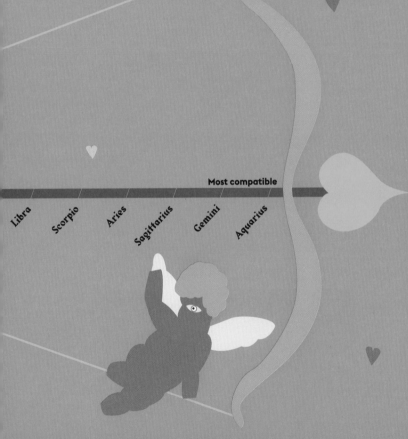

Most compatible

Libra   Scorpio   Aries   Sagittarius   Gemini   Aquarius

The

Aquari

II.

us

Deep Dive

In this section, dive deeper into the ways in which your Sun sign might be driving you or holding you back, and start to think about how you might use this knowledge to inform your path.

The
Aquarius
home

The Aquarius home is likely to reflect a love of the modern and futuristic. Contemporary materials, shiny surfaces, minimalist in style, this is a home that's likely to showcase the interesting and innovative, full of light and air with little clutter. There's unlikely to be much in the way of antiques as these depict the old not the new, and Aquarius has little sentimentality about family heirlooms.

As an air sign depicted by the water carrier, there's also likely to be a sense of fluidity about the place, with blue colours in the decor and furnishings, or paintings of skies and seascapes on the wall. There may even be an actual water feature or aquarium filled with darting fish. Unlikely to have a home described by their friends as homely, Aquarius is more likely to opt for stripped wood or polished floors and steel-framed leather furniture; rather than luxury carpets and plush sofas. Socially minded, there's always plenty of room for visitors and guests, however, and conversations continuing late into the night. In many ways, the Aquarius home is about the people who occupy it – not its contents – which is what they most enjoy.

TOP TIPS FOR AQUARIUS SELF-CARE

★ Asking for help when you need it is not a sign of weakness.

★ Walking meditation can help keep legs strong and also eases that busy mind.

★ Remember, regular meals will help balance that flighty energy.

Self-care

Unsurprisingly for such an independently minded sign, Aquarius expects to look after themselves without much input or support from others. They are one of the least likely signs to be a hypochondriac and are seldom very much concerned about their health, often disregarding minor aches and pains. This is fine for the most part but when something doesn't resolve it can take them a while to ask for help and, because of this, sometimes things get worse than they should before they get better. Aquarius is the one who come back from a ski holiday on crutches and refuses to comply with medical advice once the cast is off. The key for Aquarius is to be a little more self-aware, which will help avoid problems escalating.

Aquarius does actually need other people from time to time, and accepting and valuing this part of human nature will actually help them look after themselves. While they recognise that, in the words of fellow Aquarian poet John Donne, 'no man is an island; every man is a piece of the continent', they don't always apply this to themselves. In accepting this humanitarian ideal, it actually becomes easier for Aquarius to look after themselves while still retaining their cherished independence.

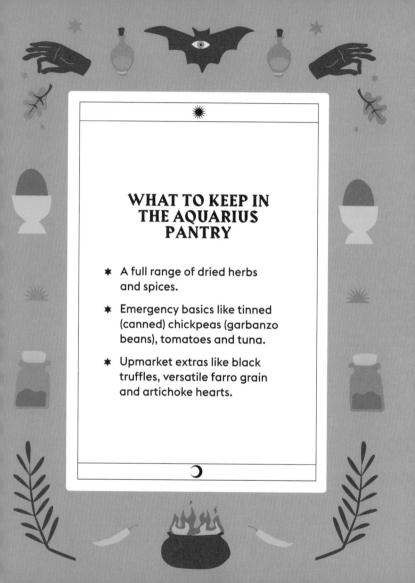

WHAT TO KEEP IN THE AQUARIUS PANTRY

* A full range of dried herbs and spices.

* Emergency basics like tinned (canned) chickpeas (garbanzo beans), tomatoes and tuna.

* Upmarket extras like black truffles, versatile farro grain and artichoke hearts.

Food
and
cooking

An Aquarius menu can be a bit unpredictable. Given to spontaneous and last-minute efforts, you can't expect adventurous Aquarius to give much headspace to something as mundane as food when they're off saving the planet – so what appears on the plate may be the result of pot luck rather than careful planning. Rustling up a meal out of what's in the fridge could result in quite an unexpected and surprising concoction and if one ingredient is missing, whatever's available to hand may be substituted instead – pasta for rice, for example – with interesting results. An Aquarius meal is often something of a novel experience.

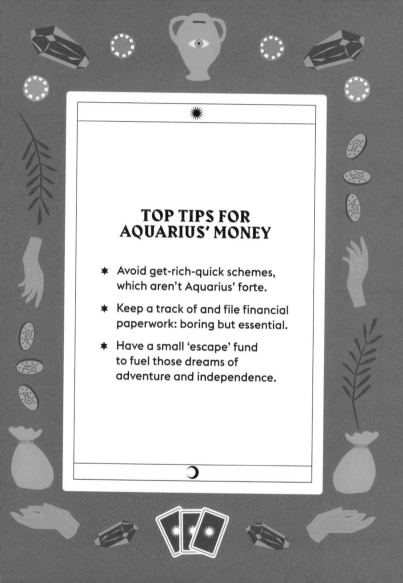

TOP TIPS FOR AQUARIUS' MONEY

★ Avoid get-rich-quick schemes, which aren't Aquarius' forte.

★ Keep a track of and file financial paperwork: boring but essential.

★ Have a small 'escape' fund to fuel those dreams of adventure and independence.

How Aquarius handles money

Given they are possibly one of the least money-minded signs, Aquarius can be surprisingly successful because they like money as a means to an end, allowing them all the possibilities of financial independence. Aquarius' combination of people skills and innovation often means their entrepreneurial ideas create wealth, almost as a by-product rather than a primary aim. They also make money work for them in interesting ways and are more likely to invest in a crazy scheme to which they've given massive thought, than to stuff cash under the proverbial mattress. Using data from the Forbes rich list, MSN ranked Aquarius second (to Leo) in their list of 100 richest people in the world. Closer to home, Aquarius is unlikely to struggle with money as it's just another commodity to which they have no emotional connection, which liberates their attitude and probably accounts for their success with it. Aquarius also likes to give back and is often generous to charities, too.

How Aquarius handles the boss

Answering to a boss can sometimes be tricky for independent types like Aquarius; and working in a team may require a tad more thought and accommodation than may come naturally to many of them. Because of their commitment to the bigger picture, however, once they see that ensuring the greater good of the whole company is an aim worth working towards, they might find it easier to take on board what their boss needs them to do.

Often valued for their unpredictable and sometimes innovative approach to problem-solving, the boss may look to an Aquarius employee for exactly this talent and allocate work that can be done to support it, even enabling them to work more independently as long as the details are mutually understood. Communication, very much Aquarius' forte, is a great tool here and especially valued when used to get things done.

While Aquarius embraces hard work and will put in long hours to go the extra mile, they have to believe it's worthwhile and will contribute to some future progress in order to do so.

TOP TIPS TO
HANDLE THE BOSS

★ Keep communicating,
  especially if you want to
  do something differently.

★ Always work with the boss to
  negotiate more independence
  in the workplace.

★ Remember that rules are
  devised for the greater good
  of the whole company, not
  to inhibit Aquarius!

TOP TIPS FOR AN EASIER LIFE

* If you want to save the planet through recycling, have a system that's easy for everyone to use.

* Use a communal calendar to keep track of social activities.

* Remember that it's everyone's job, including yours to keep the bath cleaned.

What is Aquarius like to live with?

'Live and let live' could have been a motto written by Aquarius and, for them, these words lie at the heart of their attitude when it comes to co-habiting. It's also the attitude they expect from their housemates, whether lovers or friends, which might cause a little friction if not everyone is on the same page.

Aquarius is often away, either working long hours or just travelling for pleasure in some far-flung place. As a result they are used to fending for themselves and getting on with all sorts of different people. The upside to this is that they are generally very tolerant and open to discussion, so household problems are easily aired and solved. When they are around, Aquarians are very social, either spending hours at the kitchen table discussing the ways of the world with their lover or inviting a motley crew over to do the same.

Domesticity may be approached in a rather whirlwind way or methodically: Aquarius is too unpredictable to be sure. They may need the occasional prompt, but it will get done because at heart Aquarius does likes a degree of order and organisation.

How to handle a break-up

Aquarius doesn't much like the emotional extremes – their own or their ex's – that tend to occur with a break-up and will often continue with a relationship long after it's over (or wait until their lover does the breaking-up) in order to avoid potential heartbreak. Their response can be unpredictable, but their humanitarian heart means that they never enjoy hurting others and they also resent the sheer time and emotional energy it takes for the heart to heal. This also explains why Aquarius is often slow to commit, preferring to be friends for a long time before declaring their love in the first place. What Aquarius also expects is that they can be friends afterwards, once the dust has settled, and that's not always easy for an ex to tolerate, regardless of who called it off.

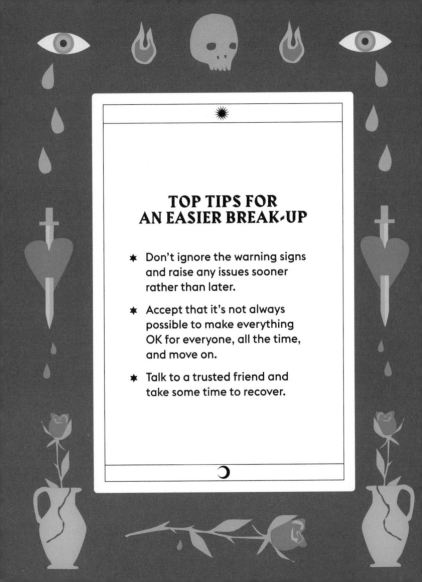

TOP TIPS FOR AN EASIER BREAK-UP

★ Don't ignore the warning signs and raise any issues sooner rather than later.

★ Accept that it's not always possible to make everything OK for everyone, all the time, and move on.

★ Talk to a trusted friend and take some time to recover.

How Aquarius wants to be loved

The simplest answer to this question might appear to be: at a distance. There's a cool, reserved aspect to Aquarius' emotions that can give off quite a detached vibe, making it tricky for those who care deeply about them to work out how best to get close. Over-attention smacks of claustrophobia to many born under Aquarius, and their dislike of this can be misinterpreted, so any loving has to acknowledge their independent nature. Labelling Aquarius as a commitment-phobe wouldn't necessarily be accurate: although their behaviour can often look like it, it could be a mistake to take it at face value. Communication, which is Aquarius' main suit, can be helpful here and they appreciate a straightforward approach.

Friendship is huge to Aquarius, and their friends are often so diverse, eccentric and wide-ranging in age, cultural style and personality it would be hard to work out what anyone had in common – or what type of person Aquarius is attracted to. One of the problems with Aquarius' inquiring mind and general friendliness and interest in someone is that it can create expectations. This can lead anyone who is the focus of Aquarius' attention to think this interest is of a romantic kind. It may take a little longer to be sure!

If those trying to romance Aquarius find their behaviour perplexing, Aquarius is also perplexed when their relationships are problematic, because they – of course – perceive themselves as entirely straightforward. They want someone to love them who is as independent as they are, but available. An active disposition is great, but make sure that activity is as much in the mind as the body. Unpredictable behaviour is fine, as long as it's predictable when necessary. Find a common cause, but don't crowd them.

Shared interests are always a good place to start a relationship, especially with Aquarius. In fact, partnerships with Aquarius are often forged over a joint project which stimulates mental activity. This allows shyer (yes, they do exist!) Aquarians to find their feet and learn to trust that their unconditional and unconventional way of loving won't be rejected. Because often Aquarius can feel a little insecure and it's only over time that they will commit. When Aquarius makes a promise, they are likely to honour it. They are generous and tolerant and happy to build a future with someone who sparks their mind as well as their body.

TOP TIPS FOR
LOVING AQUARIUS

* They offer unconditional love
  but tend to expect the same
  in return.

* Be honest and upfront about
  your feelings and respect their
  humanitarian values.

* Surprise them: they love
  the unexpected.

Aquarius' sex life

Remember all those adjectives applied to Aquarius like unpredictable, experimental and unconventional? Yup, they apply here in the bedroom, too, and there's no doubt that for Aquarius, sex can be an intense, exciting and passionate affair – and even at times a little kinky. But here's the paradox, Aquarius can also be rather serious and thoughtful about things and although once they're in bed they're seldom cautious, it can take them a while to get there. There's nothing overtly flirtatious about Aquarius' sexual style. In fact, their sex life often starts in their head, because the primary stimulation for Aquarius can be somewhat intellectual, taking quite a while to reach the physical.

The one-night stand is unusual for Aquarius, as they prefer to get to know their lover's mind first. To their lover, this can look like the slow burn of caution, but it is usually more to do with Aquarius' tendency to focus on the individual they wish to get to know. Despite initial appearences, they are by no means a conventional lover. Once involved, Aquarius may surprise their lover with highly erotic talk as part of their repertoire and they might also suggest role play, new sexual positions and unusual locations.

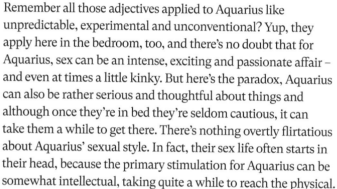

Give

III.

Me More

Your Sun sign never shows you the whole picture. In this section, learn how to read the nuances of your birth chart and discover a whole new level of astrological insight.

Your birth chart

Your birth chart is a snapshot of a particular moment, in a particular place, at the precise moment of your birth and is therefore completely individual to you. It's like a blueprint, a map, a statement of occurrence, spelling out possible traits and influences – but it isn't your destiny. It is just a symbolic tool to which you can refer, based on the position of the planets at the time of your birth. If you can't get to an astrologer, these days anyone can get their birth chart prepared in minutes online (see page 108 for a list of websites and apps that will do it for you). Even if you don't know your exact time of birth, just knowing the date and place of birth can create the beginnings of a useful template.

Remember, nothing is intrinsically good or bad in astrology and there is no explicit timing or forecasting: it's more a question of influences and how these might play out positively or negatively. And if we have some insight, and some tools with which to approach, see or interpret our circumstances and surroundings, this gives us something to work with.

When you are reading your birth chart, it's useful to first understand the tools of astrology available to you; not only the astrological signs and what they represent, but also the 10 planets referred to in astrology and their individual characteristics, along with the 12 houses and what they mean. Individually, these tools of astrology are of passing interest, but when you start to see how they might sit in juxtaposition to each other, then the bigger picture becomes more accessible and we begin to gain insights that can be useful to us.

Broadly speaking, each of the planets suggests a different type of energy, the astrological signs propose the various ways in which that energy might be expressed, while the houses represent areas of experience in which this expression might operate.

Next to bring into the picture are the positions of the signs at four key points: the ascendant, or rising sign, and its opposite, the descendant; and the midheaven and its opposite, the IC, not to mention the different aspects created by congregations of signs and planets.

It is now possible to see how subtle the reading of a birth chart might be and how it is infinite in its variety, and highly specific to an individual. With this information, and a working understanding of the symbolic meaning and influences of the signs, planets and houses of your unique astrological profile, you can begin to use these tools to help with decision-making and other aspects of life.

Reading your chart

If you have your birth chart prepared, either by hand or via an online program, you will see a circle divided into 12 segments, with information clustered at various points indicating the position of each zodiac sign, in which segment it appears and at what degree. Irrespective of the features that are relevant to the individual, each chart follows the same pattern when it comes to interpretation.

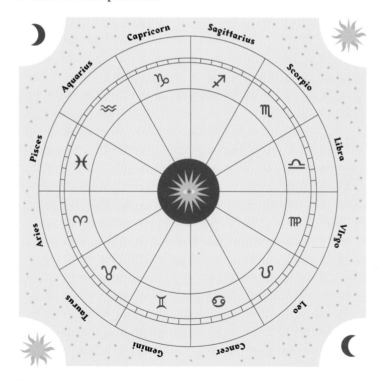

Given the time of birth, the place of birth and the position of the planets at that moment, the birth chart, sometimes called a natal horoscope, is drawn up.

If you consider the chart as a clock face, the first house (see pages 95–99 for the astrological houses) begins at the 9, and it is from this point that, travelling anti-clockwise the chart is read from the first house, through the 12 segments of the chart to the twelfth.

The beginning point, the 9, is also the point at which the Sun rises on your life, giving you your ascendant, or rising sign, and opposite to this, at the 3 of the clock face, is your descendant sign. The midheaven point of your chart, the MC, is at 12, and its opposite, the IC, at 6 (see pages 101–102).

Understanding the significance of the characteristics of the astrological signs and the planets, their particular energies, their placements and their aspects to each other can be helpful in understanding ourselves and our relationships with others. In day-to-day life, too, the changing configuration of planets and their effects are much more easily understood with a basic knowledge of astrology, as are the recurring patterns that can sometimes strengthen and sometimes delay opportunities and possibilities. Working with, rather than against, these trends can make life more manageable and, in the last resort, more successful.

The Moon effect

If your Sun sign represents your consciousness, your life force and your individual will, then the Moon represents that side of your personality that you tend to keep rather secret or hidden. This is the realm of instinct, intuition, creativity and the unconscious, which can take you places emotionally that are sometimes hard to understand. This is what brings great subtlety and nuance to a person, way beyond just their Sun sign. So you may have your Sun in Aquarius, and all that means, but this might be countered by a strongly empathetic and feeling Moon in Cancer; or you may have your Sun in open-hearted Leo, but a Moon in Aquarius with all its rebellious, emotional detachment.

Phases of the Moon

The Moon orbits the Earth, taking roughly 28 days to do so. How much of the Moon we see is determined by how much of the Sun's light it reflects, giving us the impression that it waxes, or grows, and wanes. When the Moon is new, to us, only a sliver of it is illuminated. As it waxes, it reflects more light and moves from a crescent, to a waxing crescent to a first quarter; then it moves to a waxing gibbous Moon, to a full Moon. Then the Moon begins to wane through a waning gibbous, to a last quarter, and then the cycle begins again. All of this occurs over four weeks. When we have two full Moons in any one calendar month, the second is called a blue Moon.

Each month the Moon also moves through an astrological sign, as we know from our personal birth charts. This, too, will yield information – a Moon in Scorpio can have a very different effect to one in Capricorn – and depending on our personal charts, this can have a shifting influence each month. For example, if the Moon in your birth chart is in Virgo, then when the actual Moon moves into Virgo, this will have an additional influence. Read the characteristics of the signs for further information (see pages 12–17).

The Moon's cycle has an energetic effect, which we can see quite easily on the ocean tides. Astrologically, because the Moon is both a fertility symbol and attuned to our deeper psychological side, we can use this to focus more profoundly and creatively on aspects of life that are important to us.

Eclipses

Generally speaking, an eclipse covers up and prevents light being shed on a situation. Astrologically speaking, this will depend on where the Sun or Moon is positioned in relation to other planets at the time of an eclipse. So if a solar eclipse is in Gemini, there will be a Geminian influence or an influence on Geminis.

Hiding, or shedding, light on an area of our lives is an invitation to pay attention to it. Eclipses are generally about beginnings or endings, which is why our ancestors saw them as portents, important signs to be taken notice of. As it is possible to know when an eclipse is forthcoming, these are charted astronomically; consequently, their astrological significance can be assessed and acted upon ahead of time.

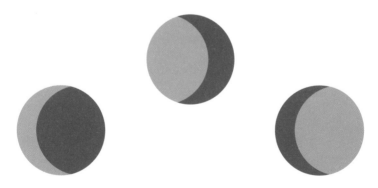

The 10 planets

For the purpose of astrology (but not for astronomy, because the Sun is really a star) we talk about 10 planets, and each astrological sign has a ruling planet, with Mercury, Venus and Mars each being assigned two. The characteristics of each planet describe those influences that can affect signs, all of which information feeds into the interpretation of a birth chart.

The Moon

This sign is an opposing principle to the Sun, forming a pair, and it represents the feminine, symbolising containment and receptivity, how we react most instinctively and with feeling.

Rules the sign of Cancer.

The Sun

The Sun represents the masculine, and is seen as the energy that sparks life, which suggests a paternal energy in our birth chart. It also symbolises our self or essential being, and our purpose.

Rules the sign of Leo.

Mercury

Mercury is the planet of communication and symbolises our urge to make sense of, understand and communicate our thoughts through words.

Rules the signs of Gemini and Virgo.

Venus

The planet of love is all about
attraction, connection and pleasure
and in a female chart it symbolises
her style of femininity, while in a male
chart it represents his ideal partner.

Rules the signs of Taurus and Libra.

Mars

This planet symbolises pure energy
(Mars was, after all, the god of War)
but it also tells you in which areas
you're most likely to be assertive,
aggressive or to take risks.

Rules the signs of Aries and Scorpio.

Saturn

Saturn is sometimes called the wise teacher or taskmaster of astrology, symbolising lessons learnt and limitations, showing us the value of determination, tenacity and resilience.

Rules the sign of Capricorn.

Jupiter

The planet Jupiter is the largest in our solar system and symbolises bounty and benevolence, all that is expansive and jovial. Like the sign it rules, it's also about moving away from the home on journeys and exploration.

Rules the sign of Sagittarius.

Uranus

This planet symbolises the unexpected, new ideas and innovation, and the urge to tear down the old and usher in the new. The downside can mark an inability to fit in and consequently the feeling of being an outsider.

Rules the sign of Aquarius.

Pluto

Aligned to Hades (*Pluto* in Latin), the god of the underworld or death, this planet exerts a powerful force that lies below the surface and which, in its most negative form, can represent obsessions and compulsive behaviour.

Rules the sign of Scorpio.

Neptune

Linked to the sea, this is about what lies beneath, underwater and too deep to be seen clearly. Sensitive, intuitive and artistic, it also symbolises the capacity to love unconditionally, to forgive and forget.

Rules the sign of Pisces.

The four elements

Further divisions of the 12 astrological signs into the four elements of earth, fire, air and water yield other characteristics. This comes from ancient Greek medicine, where the body was considered to be made up of four bodily fluids or 'humours'. These four humours – blood, yellow bile, black bile and phlegm – corresponded to the four temperaments of sanguine, choleric, melancholic and phlegmatic, to the four seasons of the year, spring, summer, autumn, winter, and the four elements of air, fire, earth and water.

Related to astrology, these symbolic qualities cast further light on characteristics of the different signs. Carl Jung also used them in his psychology, and we still refer to people as earthy, fiery, airy or wet in their approach to life, while sometimes describing people as 'being in their element'. In astrology, those Sun signs that share the same element are said to have an affinity, or an understanding, with each other.

Like all aspects of astrology, there is always a positive and a negative, and a knowledge of any 'shadow side' can be helpful in terms of self-knowledge and what we may need to enhance or balance out, particularly in our dealings with others.

Air

GEMINI ✱ LIBRA ✱ AQUARIUS

The realm of ideas is
where these air signs excel.
Perceptive and visionary and
able to see the big picture,
there is a very reflective
quality to air signs that helps
to vent situations. Too much
air, however, can dissipate
intentions, so Gemini might
be indecisive, Libra has a
tendency to sit on the fence,
while Aquarius can be
very disengaged.

Fire

ARIES ✱ LEO ✱ SAGITTARIUS

There is a warmth and energy
to these signs, a positive
approach, spontaneity
and enthusiasm that can
be inspiring and very
motivational to others.
The downside is that Aries
has a tendency to rush in
headfirst, Leo can have a need
for attention and Sagittarius
can tend to talk it up but
not deliver.

Earth

TAURUS ✷ VIRGO ✷ CAPRICORN

Characteristically, these
signs enjoy sensual pleasure,
relishing food and other
physical satisfactions, and
they like to feel grounded,
preferring to base their ideas
in facts. The downside is that
Taureans can be stubborn,
Virgos can be pernickety and
Capricorns can veer towards
a dogged conservatism.

Water

CANCER ✷ SCORPIO ✷ PISCES

Water signs are very
responsive, like the tide
ebbing and flowing, and
can be very perceptive
and intuitive, sometimes
uncannily so because of their
ability to feel. The downside
is – watery enough – a
tendency to feel swamped,
and then Cancer can be both
tenacious and self-protective,
Pisces chameleon-like in
their attention and Scorpio
unpredictable and intense.

Cardinal, fixed and mutable signs

In addition to the 12 signs being divided into four elements, they can also be grouped into three different ways in which their energies may act or react, giving further depth to each sign's particular characteristics.

Cardinal

ARIES ✻ CANCER ✻ LIBRA ✻ CAPRICORN

These are action planets, with an energy that takes the initiative and gets things started. Aries has the vision, Cancer the feelings, Libra the contacts and Capricorn the strategy.

Fixed

TAURUS ✴ LEO ✴ SCORPIO ✴ AQUARIUS

Slower but more determined, these signs work to progress and maintain those initiatives that the cardinal signs have fired up. Taurus offers physical comfort, Leo loyalty, Scorpio emotional support and Aquarius sound advice. You can count on fixed signs, but they tend to resist change.

Mutable

GEMINI ✴ VIRGO ✴ SAGITTARIUS ✴ PISCES

Adaptable and responsive to new ideas, places and people, mutable signs have a unique ability to adjust to their surroundings. Gemini is mentally agile, Virgo is practical and versatile, Sagittarius visualises possibilities and Pisces is responsive to change.

The 12 houses

The birth chart is divided into 12 houses, which represent separate areas and functions of your life. When you are told you have something in a specific house – for example, Libra (balance) in the fifth house (creativity and sex) – it creates a way of interpreting the influences that can arise and are particular to how you might approach an aspect of your life.

Each house relates to a Sun sign, and in this way each is represented by some of the characteristics of that sign, which is said to be its natural ruler.

Three of these houses are considered to be mystical, relating to our interior, psychic world: the fourth (home), eighth (death and regeneration) and twelfth (secrets).

1st House

THE SELF

RULED BY ARIES

This house symbolises the self: you, who you are and how you represent yourself, your likes, dislikes and approach to life. It also represents how you see yourself and what you want in life.

2nd House

POSSESSIONS

RULED BY TAURUS

The second house symbolises your possessions, what you own, including money; how you earn or acquire your income; and your material security and the physical things you take with you as you move through life.

3rd House

COMMUNICATION

RULED BY GEMINI

This house is about communication and mental attitude, primarily how you express yourself. It's also about how you function within your family, and how you travel to school or work, and includes how you think, speak, write and learn.

4th House

HOME

RULED BY CANCER

This house is about your roots and your home or homes, present, past and future, so it includes both your childhood and current domestic set-up. It's also about what home and security represents to you.

5th House

CREATIVITY

RULED BY LEO

Billed as the house of creativity and play, this also includes sex, and relates to the creative urge, the libido, in all its manifestations. It's also about speculation in finance and love, games, fun and affection: affairs of the heart.

6th House

HEALTH

RULED BY VIRGO

This house is related to health: our own physical and emotional health, and how robust it is; but also those we care for, look after or provide support to – from family members to work colleagues.

7th House

PARTNERSHIPS

RULED BY LIBRA

The opposite of the first house, this reflects shared goals and intimate partnerships, our choice of life partner and how successful our relationships might be. It also reflects partnerships and adversaries in our professional world.

8th House

REGENERATION

RULED BY SCORPIO

For death, read regeneration or spiritual transformation: this house also reflects legacies and what you inherit after death, in personality traits or materially. And because regeneration requires sex, it's also about sex and sexual emotions.

9th House

TRAVEL

RULED BY SAGITTARIUS

The house of long-distance travel and exploration, this is also about the broadening of the mind that travel can bring, and how that might express itself. It also reflects the sending out of ideas, which can come about from literary effort or publication.

11th House

FRIENDSHIPS

RULED BY AQUARIUS

The eleventh house is about friendship groups and acquaintances, vision and ideas, and is less about immediate gratification but more concerning longer-term dreams and how these might be realised through our ability to work harmoniously with others.

12th House

SECRETS

RULED BY PISCES

Considered the most spiritual house, it is also the house of the unconscious, of secrets and of what might lie hidden, the metaphorical skeleton in the closet. It also reflects the secret ways we might self-sabotage or imprison our own efforts by not exploring them.

10th House

ASPIRATIONS

RULED BY CAPRICORN

This represents our aspiration and status, how we'd like to be elevated in public standing (or not), our ambitions, image and what we'd like to attain in life, through our own efforts.

The ascendant

Otherwise known as your rising sign, this is the sign of the zodiac that appears at the horizon as dawn breaks on the day of your birth, depending on your location in the world and time of birth. This is why knowing your time of birth is a useful factor in astrology, because your 'rising sign' yields a lot of information about those aspects of your character that are more on show, how you present yourself and how you are seen by others. So, even if you are a Sun Aquarius, but have Cancer rising, you may be seen as someone who is maternal, with a noticeable commitment to the domestic life in one way or another. Knowing your own ascendant – or that of another person – will often help explain why there doesn't seem to be such a direct correlation between their personality and their Sun sign.

As long as you know your time of birth and where you were born, working out your ascendant using an online tool or app is very easy (see page 108). Just ask your mum or other family members, or check your birth certificate (in those countries that include a birth time). If the astrological chart were a clock face, the ascendant is at the 9 o'clock position.

The descendant

The descendant gives an indication of a possible life partner, based on the idea that opposites attract. Once you know your ascendant, the descendant is easy to work out as it is always six signs away: for example, if your ascendant is Virgo, your descendant is Pisces. If the astrological chart were a clock face, the descendant would be at the 3 o'clock position.

The midheaven (MC)

Also included in the birth chart is the position of the midheaven or MC (from the Latin, *medium coeli*, meaning middle of the heavens), which indicates your attitude towards your work, career and professional standing. If the astrological chart were a clock face, the MC would be at the 12 o'clock position.

The IC

Finally, your IC (from the Latin, *imum coeli*, meaning the lowest part of the heavens) indicates your attitude towards your home and family, and is also related to the end of your life. Your IC will be six signs away from your MC: for example, if your MC is Aquarius, your IC is Leo. If the astrological chart were a clock face, the IC is at the 6 o'clock position.

Saturn return

Saturn is one of the slower-moving planets, taking around 28 years to complete its orbit around the Sun and return to the place it occupied at the time of your birth. This return can last between two to three years and be very noticeable in the period coming up to our thirtieth and sixtieth birthdays, often considered to be significant 'milestone' birthdays.

Because the energy of Saturn is sometimes experienced as demanding, this isn't always an easy period of life. A wise teacher or a hard taskmaster, some consider the Saturn effect as 'cruel to be kind' in the way that many good teachers can be, keeping us on track like a rigorous personal trainer.

Everyone experiences their Saturn return relevant to their circumstances, but it is a good time to take stock, let go of the stuff in your life that no longer serves you, revise your expectations while being unapologetic about what you would like to include more of in your life. So if you are experiencing or anticipating this life event, embrace and work with it because what you learn now – about yourself, mainly – is worth knowing, however turbulent it might be, and can pay dividends in how you manage the next 28 years!

Mercury retrograde

Even those with little interest in astrology often take notice when the planet Mercury is retrograde. Astrologically, retrogrades are periods when planets are stationary but, as we continue to move forwards, Mercury 'appears' to move backwards. There is a shadow period either side of a retrograde period, when it could be said to be slowing down or speeding up, which can also be a little turbulent. Generally speaking, the advice is not to make any important moves related to communication on a retrograde and, even if a decision is made, know that it's likely to change.

Given that Mercury is the planet of communication, you can immediately see why there are concerns about its retrograde status and its link to communication failures – of the old-fashioned sort when the post office loses a letter, or the more modern technological variety when your computer crashes

– causing problems. Mercury retrograde can also affect travel, with delays in flights or train times, traffic jams or collisions. Mercury also influences personal communications: listening, speaking, being heard (or not), and can cause confusion or arguments. It can also affect more formal agreements, like contracts between buyer and seller.

These retrograde periods occur three to four times a year, lasting for roughly three weeks, with a shadow period either side. The dates in which it happens also means it occurs within a specific astrological sign. If, for example, it occurs between 25 October and 15 November, its effect would be linked to the characteristics of Scorpio. In addition, those Sun sign Scorpios, or those with Scorpio in significant placements in their chart, may also experience a greater effect.

Mercury retrograde dates are easy to find from an astrological table, or ephemeris, and online. These can be used in order to avoid planning events that might be affected around these times. How Mercury retrograde may affect you more personally requires knowledge of your birth chart and an understanding of its more specific combination of influences with the signs and planets in your chart.

If you are going to weather a Mercury retrograde more easily, be aware that glitches can occur so, to some extent, expect delays and double-check details. Stay positive if postponements occur and consider this period an opportunity to slow down, review or reconsider ideas in your business or your personal life. Use the time to correct mistakes or reshape plans, preparing for when any stuck energy can shift and you can move forward again more smoothly.

Further reading

Astrology Decoded (2013) by Sue Merlyn Farebrother; published by Rider

Astrology for Dummies (2007) by Rae Orion; published by Wiley Publishing

Chart Interpretation Handbook: Guidelines for Understanding the Essentials of the Birth Chart (1990) by Stephen Arroyo; published by CRCS Publications

Jung's Studies in Astrology (2018) by Liz Greene; published by RKP

The Only Astrology Book You'll Ever Need (2012) by Joanne Woolfolk; published by Taylor Trade

Websites

astro.com

astrologyzone.com

jessicaadams.com

shelleyvonstrunkel.com

Apps

Astrostyle

Co-Star

Susan Miller's Astrology Zone

The Daily Horoscope

The Pattern

Time Passages

Acknowledgements

Particular thanks are due to my trusty team of Taureans. Firstly, to Kate Pollard, Publishing Director at Hardie Grant, for her passion for beautiful books and for commissioning this series. And to Bex Fitzsimons for all her good natured and conscientious editing. And finally to Evi O. Studio, whose illustration and design talents have produced small works of art. With such a star-studded team, these books can only shine and for that, my thanks.

About the author

Stella Andromeda has been studying astrology for over 30 years, believing that a knowledge of the constellations of the skies and their potential for psychological interpretation can be a useful tool. This extension of her study into book form makes modern insights about the ancient wisdom of the stars easily accessible, sharing her passion that reflection and self-knowledge only empowers us in life. With her sun in Taurus, Aquarius ascendant and Moon in Cancer, she utilises earth, air and water to inspire her own astrological journey.

Published in 2019 by Hardie Grant Books,
an imprint of Hardie Grant Publishing

Hardie Grant Books (London)
5th & 6th Floors
52–54 Southwark Street
London, SE1 1UN

Hardie Grant Books (Melbourne)
Building 1, 658 Church Street
Richmond, Victoria 3121

hardiegrantbooks.com

British Library Cataloguing-in-Publication Data. A catalogue record
for this book is available from the British Library.

Aquarius
ISBN: 9781784882600

20 19 18 17 16 15 14 13 12

Publishing Director: Kate Pollard
Junior Editor: Bex Fitzsimons
Art Direction and Illustrations: Evi O. Studio
Editor: Wendy Hobson
Production Controller: Sinead Hering

Colour reproduction by p2d
Printed and bound in China by Leo Paper Products Ltd.